For my wife, Heather

First published in Great Britain in 1999 by
Conran Octopus Ltd
37 Shelton Street, London WC2H 9HN
A part of Octopus Publishing Group

ISBN 1 84091 009 7

Managing Editor Kate Bell
Editorial Assistant Tanya Robinson
Copy Editor Norma MacMillan
Editorial Consultant Jenni Muir

Art Editor Alison Fenton
Stylist Wei Tang
Food for Photography Meg Jansz
Typesetting Olivia Norton

Picture Research Liz Boyd
Production Julian Deeming

British Library Cataloguing-in-Publication Data
A catalogue record for this book is available from
the British Library
Printed in Hong Kong

Both metric and imperial measurements are given
in this book. Use either all metric or all imperial
as the two are not necessarily interchangeable.

Page 1 *Mango Sorbet (page 106)*
Pages 2–3 *Mother-in-law's Eyes (page 107)*
Pages 4–5 *Married Prawns (page 32)*

street café

brazil

Michael Bateman

Photography by Jeremy Hopley

conran
OCTOPUS

Contents

Introduction

Brazil is the land of exuberant Carnival and the insistent rhythm of the samba. Its colourful people love the pleasures of life, music, dance and food. Especially food. From the tropics of the Amazon north, which yield a cornucopia of exotic fruits, to the gaucho south where they rear meat, Brazilians enjoy a rich and varied cuisine. Nowhere is this more evident than in this huge country's street food. At any public event, food sellers materialize, peddling everything from freshly simmered corn-on-the-cob to coloured hard-boiled eggs.

Brazil has been a melting pot of food cultures from the sixteenth century onwards, a fusion of the food of the native Indians, the Portuguese colonizers and African slaves. Later, in the nineteenth century, other waves of immigrants added their contributions, first Italians and Spanish, then Poles and Lebanese and, more recently, Japanese. São Paulo, one of the world's biggest cities, with a population of 17 million, boasts the largest Japanese community outside Japan, and is home to literally thousands of *sushi* bars. And Italian pizza and pasta have become universal fare both in homes and in cafés.

Brazil is the largest country in Latin America, on a par with the United States in terms of size and population. The diversity of climate from north to south equates with the differences between the damp Loire Valley and the steaming rain forests and arid deserts of West and Central Africa. So in the south; you find cowboy types cooking steak on barbecues (the *churrascaria*), while in the north, the meat eaten is more likely to be *carne de sol* or *carne seco* (beef salted and dried in the sun). In the north, though, they enjoy a wealth of Amazon fish, wild game from the forest, vegetables such as chayote and jícama, and exotic fruits such as *graviola* (the succulent custard apple), *jabuticaba* (a cherry-sized acid fruit with a jellied texture), breadfruit, jackfruit and carambola or star fruit, not to mention papaya, mango, pineapple, guava and passion fruit.

Of all the fruit and vegetables that Brazil produces and exports none are more important than beans. Brazil is the world's largest grower and the biggest consumer. Black ones, brown ones, red and white ones. The small black beans *(feijão preto)* are the most prized. Beans and rice are eaten by most families every day, and the national dish (which Rio lays claim to) is *feijoada*, a rich, liquid stew of black beans in which half a dozen or more kinds of meat are submerged. *Feijoada* is colourfully served with white rice, butter-yellow *farofa* (the toasted flour milled from cassava), green stir-fried kale and rounds of sliced orange. It is traditionally preceded by a searingly strong rum sour called *caipirinha*, made with chopped limes crushed with sugar.

Brazilian food might have been a modest cuisine had it not been for the contribution made by the Africans, former slaves. Emancipated in the 1880s, they have made Bahia, their homeland in the north-east of Brazil, a by-word for imaginative cooking. What we see in Bahia is an early example of fusion cooking. The Portuguese came to Brazil, annexing the produce of the indigenous Indians – limes, avocados, sweetcorn, sweet potatoes, pumpkins, pineapples and peanuts. And for their part the Portuguese brought European foods, rice and sugar, olives and olive oil, coriander (the universal Brazilian herb) and, above all, the pig, and thus cured hams and sausages and lard for cooking.

The Africans in their turn introduced several kinds of palm from West Africa, one producing palm nut oil *(dendê)*, a thick, reddish, highly saturated oil that contributes perfume and flavour to any dish cooked with it. Another palm, the coconut palm, provides its multi-purpose nuts which contain a liquid *(água de coco)* that is such a refreshing and cooling drink on a hot day. The white grated flesh and the milk made from it feature in both savoury and sweet dishes. And, since the hot north-east is alien to the growing of wheat, the Africans, needing a starchy base for subsistence, brought over cassava, a hairy, white-fleshed root as thick as a mug. The flour when toasted is called *farofa*, and is sprinkled like a condiment on many dishes.

So it was that, when these several food cultures and all these disparate ingredients met, there was a gastronomic 'big bang' and *Cozinha Baiana* (Bahaian cuisine) was the result. The most popular dishes are based on seafood and shellfish – fish soups (with coconut milk, lime juice, coriander and chillies), simple fish stews *(moqueca)* with sliced onion, tomatoes and green peppers, dyed yellow with *dendê* oil, and the local speciality, baked stuffed crab, *recheadas de siri*.

Hot chillies are in evidence here, usually incorporated in the food, while in other parts of Brazil freshly made hot chilli sauces or *salsas* are always served at the table. They are mostly made from the *malagueta* chilli, a witheringly hot, very small variety native to Brazil.

Sweet dishes are adored in Brazil and served at every meal. A breakfast spread in Le Meridien hotel in Copacabana offers not only a dozen ripe tropical fruits, but rich caramel *pudim*, coconut flan *(quindão)*, cooling *manjar blanco* (a delicious wedge of blancmange made with coconut milk), succulent breads made with cornmeal, banana and coconut, and unusual preserves called *cocadas* – caramelized beetroot, carrot, pineapple, mixtures of pumpkin and coconut, guava paste, quince paste.

The recipes chosen for this book only begin to touch on a wide-ranging, vibrant and exciting cuisine that is Brazil's. Read, taste, enjoy.

Prawn Frittata

Frigideira de Camarão

This is similar to the Italian frittata of oven-baked scrambled eggs. A frigideira *though, in spite of the way it sounds, is not a cold dish, the* frigideira *being a heavy iron frying pan which can be used equally on top of the stove or in the oven. Unusually, baking powder is mixed with the beaten eggs. A deliciously savoury* frigideira *is also made with salt cod (de-salted by soaking overnight), cooked as below, or rehydrated* carne de sol *(salted dried meat) or even green cashew nuts.* **Serves 4**

500 g/1 lb 2 oz peeled raw prawns

1 onion *finely chopped*

1 green pepper *seeded and diced*

olive oil for frying

1 large tomato *skinned, seeded and diced*

2 sprigs of fresh coriander *chopped*

3 tablespoons first pressing coconut milk (see page 13)

butter for greasing

6 free-range eggs

½ teaspoon baking powder

For the marinade:

juice of 1 lime

2 garlic cloves *crushed then chopped*

sea salt and freshly ground black pepper

To serve:

boiled long-grain white rice

1 Preheat the oven to 190°C/375°F/gas 5.

2 Marinate the prawns in the lime juice, garlic, salt and pepper for 30 minutes.

3 Fry the onion and green pepper in a little olive oil until soft. Add the tomato, coriander and coconut milk and simmer until the mixture begins to thicken.

4 Stir in the prawns and heat through to incorporate the flavours.

5 Butter an oven dish of a suitable size (unless you have used an ovenproof iron frying pan) and transfer the prawn mixture to it. Beat the eggs with the baking powder, adding salt to taste, and pour over the prawns. Bake for 30–40 minutes or until set.

6 Serve with steaming hot boiled white rice.

Mussel Stew

Moqueca de Sururú

This is a dish familiar the world over, but, inevitably, in Brazil it is enhanced by the sweet and sour flavours of coconut milk and lime juice. **Serves 4**

I kg/2¼ lb mussels

200 g/7 oz onion *thinly sliced*

200 g/7 oz tomatoes *skinned, seeded and sliced*

4 sprigs of fresh coriander *chopped*

2 garlic cloves *crushed then chopped*

juice of 2 limes

200 ml/7 fl oz coconut milk
(see page 13)

100 ml/3½ fl oz *dendê* oil
(or use olive oil)

sea salt and freshly ground
black pepper

To serve:

boiled long-grain white rice

Golden Cassava Flour
(see page 72)

1 Rinse the mussels in cold water, discarding any that are open (they are dead), broken or heavy (they may contain mud). If necessary, scrub with a brush. Holding the shells firmly between thumb and forefinger, tug off the hairy 'beards'.

2 Put the mussels in a large saucepan and add the onion, tomato, coriander, garlic, lime juice, coconut milk, oil and a seasoning of salt and pepper (when adding salt, allow for the fact that the liquor that will come from the mussels when they open is salty).

3 Put the pan on a fierce heat, cover with a lid and cook rapidly until the mussels open – a matter of only a few minutes if the pan is sufficiently hot.

4 Serve in bowls accompanied by steaming hot plain boiled rice and toasted cassava flour.

Okra and Peanut Stew

Caruru

Caruru, *from the north-east, is one of the most African and most traditional of Brazilian dishes. It combines okra with both dried and fresh prawns, and a thickening of peanuts and cashew nuts, to make a tasty, glutinous dish to serve with Coconut Rice (page 77). The dish is richer if you use fish stock rather than water. If you are peeling your own prawns, reserve the shells and use them to make a stock: fry them lightly in a little butter or oil, then simmer them, just covered with water, with ½ chopped onion, 1 garlic clove, a bay leaf, a few peppercorns, a pinch of paprika and some fresh coriander stems for 15 minutes; strain, squeezing all the juices from the shells. You can, of course, make a stock with fish bones instead of prawn shells. Note that dried prawns are very pungent, and although authentic, can be omitted.* **Serves 4–6**

1 Trim the okra and chop into very small pieces. Sprinkle with the lemon juice and a little salt.

2 In a food processor (or with a pestle and mortar) first grind the nuts, and then the dried prawns.

3 Heat the oil in a large frying pan and cook the onion on a moderate heat until it starts to turn yellow. Stir in the ground dried prawns and nuts and cook for a few more minutes.

4 Add the whole prawns and the ginger and cook for a few minutes, then add the fish stock or water and the okra. Simmer for 30 minutes on the lowest heat, stirring to prevent sticking and adding more water to avoid it drying out.

5 Depending on your tastes, add a few drops of *pimenta-de-cheiro* or a chilli sauce such as Tabasco diluted with a little boiling water. Sprinkle with toasted cassava flour and serve with coconut rice.

1 kg/2¼ lb okra

juice of 1 lemon

sea salt and freshly ground black pepper

100 g/3½ oz shelled peanuts (or use 55 g/2 oz peanuts and 40 g/ 1½ oz cashew nuts) *lightly toasted and skins rubbed off*

125 g/4½ oz dried prawns *chopped*

2 tablespoons *dendê* oil (or use sunflower oil)

1 onion *finely chopped*

500 g/1 lb 2 oz peeled raw prawns

1 teaspoon grated fresh ginger

250 ml/9 fl oz fish stock or water

***pimenta-de-cheiro* pickled in vinegar (or use Tabasco sauce)**

Golden Cassava Flour (see page 72)

Coconut Rice (see page 77)

Shellfish Savoury Rice

Arroz de Marisco

This typical rice dish from the north has neither the sophistication of an Italian seafood risotto nor the intensity of a Spanish arroz marinera *in which seafood flavours are absorbed while the rice is cooking. On the other hand it has the merits of simplicity, depending mainly on the excellence of the shellfish used.* **Serves 4**

1 Put the prawns and crab meat in a bowl, and toss with half the lime juice, the coriander and a seasoning of salt and pepper.

2 In a frying pan, sauté the onion in a little olive oil until soft. Stir in the tomato and tomato purée. Add the prawns and crab meat and, when very hot, add the mussels and oysters (or clams). Cover and cook until all the shells open in the steam, which will take only a few minutes.

3 Add the rest of the lime juice and check seasoning. Stir in the cooked rice and heat through until it is steaming and has absorbed the flavours of the seafood.

250 g/9 oz peeled raw prawns

250 g/9 oz white crab meat

juice of 2 limes

3 sprigs of fresh coriander *chopped*

sea salt and freshly ground black pepper

1 onion *finely chopped*

olive oil for frying

1 large tomato *skinned and seeded*

1 teaspoon tomato purée

20 mussels *scrubbed and bearded*

4 or 8 fresh oysters or clams in shell

500 g/1 lb 2 oz long-grain white rice *boiled and left to cool*

67

SIDE
DISHES

Purée of Brown Beans

Tutú à Mineira

This is the predominant dish of the Minas Gerais province where it's eaten with all pork dishes, alongside plain white rice and the universal couve *greens (Crispy Stir-fried Kale, page 73). You don't need a lot of dried beans, because they double in size as they soak.*
Serves up to 6

1 Put the beans in a saucepan and cover with fresh water. Bring to the boil, skimming off the scum that rises to the surface. (Don't add salt at this stage as it would harden the beans.) Turn down the heat and simmer for about 2 hours, or until tender. Beans vary in cooking time with quality and age, so cook longer if still hard.

2 Meanwhile, in a frying pan, cook the onion in the oil until soft. Add the green pepper and cook for a further 5 minutes. Add the garlic and cook for 1 minute. Stir in the tomatoes and cook for a few more minutes. Stir in the cassava flour together with 500 ml/18 fl oz of the liquid the beans are cooking in. Mix to a smooth paste, adding seasoning to taste.

3 Using a slotted spoon, remove the beans from their cooking liquid (which you must reserve). Purée them in a blender, in batches, adding a little of the reserved liquid to make a smooth purée.

4 In a large pan, mix together the puréed beans and the cassava flour mixture, adding enough bean cooking liquid to give a texture that is neither too stiff nor too soupy. Check the seasoning. Stand this pan in a larger pan of simmering water to prevent burning or sticking. Heat for 15 minutes so the flavours blend and the mixture thickens. You can leave it to simmer for longer, but top up with liquid as necessary.

5 Serve sprinkled with chopped coriander and spring onions.

250 g/9 oz dried small Brazilian brown beans (or use kidney beans) *soaked overnight*

1 onion *finely chopped*

2 tablespoons olive or sunflower oil

1 green pepper *seeded and chopped*

2 garlic cloves *crushed then chopped*

2 tomatoes *skinned, seeded and chopped*

75 g/3 oz cassava flour

sea salt and freshly ground black pepper

To serve:

sprig of fresh coriander *finely chopped*

bunch of spring onions *chopped*

Milk Sweet

Doce de Leite

This is a popular accompaniment to desserts, similar to clotted cream. It's sometimes eaten on bread or with cakes, and sometimes with a spoon just as it is. One common Latin-American version is made by immersing an unopened can of sweetened condensed milk in water and simmering for several hours, after which (taking care to let it cool thoroughly before opening) it will have turned to a soft toffee-like consistency. Doce de leite forms little lumps after prolonged cooking and so should be removed from the heat when it starts to brown. **Serves 6–8**

1 Put the milk and sugar in a saucepan and bring to a rapid boil, stirring with a wooden spoon until the sugar dissolves.

2 Add the vanilla pod and cinnamon. Turn down the heat to the lowest possible and simmer for about 1½ hours, stirring from time to time to prevent sticking.

3 As the water in the milk evaporates, the mixture thickens and reduces in volume. Eventually the dense sugars begin to brown and form lumps. Remove and discard the vanilla pod and cinnamon sticks. Take off the heat and leave to cool, then chill.

4 Serve chilled. *Doce de leite* will keep in the fridge for a week.

3 litres/4¼ pints milk

1 kg/2¼ lb sugar

1 vanilla pod

2 sticks cinnamon

Toffee Fudge Sweets

Brigadeiro

One of the universal children's party sweets in Brazil, this is a kind of milky toffee.
Makes about 40 pieces

1 In a non-stick saucepan, over a heat diffuser, gently heat the condensed milk with the butter, chocolate and milk. Stir with a wooden spoon until the mixture comes away from the sides of the pan.

2 Remove from the heat and add the vanilla essence.

3 On a cool buttered surface (a marble slab would be ideal) spread the mixture with a palette knife.

4 When cool enough to handle, cut the mixture into 40 pieces. With your hands, roll each into a small ball and then roll in chocolate vermicelli to coat all over.

5 If you have suitable small sweet moulds, press the toffee fudge in to shape the pieces. Lay them on a tray lined with greaseproof paper and allow to cool thoroughly and set.

2 x 450 g/15 oz cans condensed milk

20 g/¾ oz unsalted butter

3 tablespoons grated dark chocolate (with 70% cocoa solids)

100 ml/3½ fl oz milk

5 drops of pure vanilla essence

butter for greasing

chocolate vermicelli

Nut Brittle

Pé-de-Moleque

This is a street sweet sold in towns and cities alike, but it is easy enough to make at home. Use other nuts to taste, such as chopped castanha de Pará *(Brazil nuts), almonds or hazelnuts. This recipe uses the cheapest nuts —* amendoim, *or peanuts. Muscovado sugar gives a luscious, rich flavour, while white sugar lets the nuts speak for themselves.* Moleque *is a mischievous boy, urchin or beggar and his* pé *is his foot. So this is Ragamuffin's Foot.*

Makes about 1 kg/2¼ lb

500 g/1 lb 2 oz unsalted peanuts

1 kg/2¼ lb muscovado sugar or white granulated sugar

butter for greasing

1 Toast the peanuts under the grill or on a low heat in a very lightly oiled frying pan. Keep shaking the nuts so that they toast evenly. If you cook them too quickly they will burn on the outside, remaining raw inside.

2 Remove from the heat. When cool enough to handle, rub the nuts in a tea towel to loosen the flaky skins. Roughly chop the peanuts.

3 Bring 1 litre/1¾ pints water to the boil. Pour in the sugar, stirring until it dissolves. Boil rapidly and, when the syrup begins to thicken, add the peanuts. Continue boiling until the brittle is ready, stirring to prevent sticking. To test, remove a little with a wooden spoon and dip it into a bowl of cold water set beside the cooker; if the brittle hardens, it is ready. If you have a sugar thermometer, this should be the hard crack stage, 146°C/295°F.

4 While the brittle is boiling, half fill the sink with cold water. As soon as the brittle is ready, remove the pan from the heat and gently dip the base into the cold water for a few moments, to stop the cooking.

5 Pour the brittle on to two buttered flat tins, each about 30 x 20 cm/ 12 x 8 in. When almost cool, make cuts all over the surface to mark out roughly shaped pieces. When cold break the brittle along these lines.

Passion Fruit Cocktail

Batida de Maracujá

The batida *is the cousin of the* caipirinha, *a chilled white rum cocktail with freshly pressed fruit juice. The main difference between a lime* batida *and* caipirinha *is that the former is strained before serving.* Batidas *are made with every kind of fruit juice, from pineapple juice to coconut milk.* Maracujá *(passion fruit) is one of the most liked, evoking the heady scents of tropical Brazil.* **Makes 4 drinks**

1 Cut the passion fruits in half and scoop out the flesh into a sieve. Press with the back of a spoon to strain the juice from the seeds. (The seeds and skins can be heated through with a glass of water and 1 tablespoon of sugar, then strained and cooled, to make a tart sauce which you can add to a fruit salad or thicken with cornflour to serve as a sauce.)

2 Slip the ice cubes into a small plastic bag, place on a chopping board and reduce them to splinters using a rolling pin or similar.

3 Combine the *cachaça*, passion fruit juice, sugar and crushed ice, and shake well.

4 Serve in glasses you have chilled in the freezer.

8 wrinkled passion fruits

20 ice cubes

300 ml/½ pint *cachaça*

4 teaspoons caster sugar

White Rum Sour

Caipirinha

The most famous of traditional Brazilian cocktails, this is drunk before a meal to give you a kick-start. The ice is cooling, the freshness of the lime arouses the appetite and the concentration of alcohol animates conversation. Caipirinha *actually translates as 'yokel' or 'country bumpkin', perhaps indicating the rough and ready way the limes are coarsely chopped into the drink. There are literally hundreds of brands of* cachaça, *the national spirit, a white rum made from cane sugar, the best very good indeed. Modern twists are* caipirosca *with vodka instead of* cachaça, *and* caipirissima, *made with Bacardi rum.*

Makes 4 drinks

2 limes

16 ice cubes

4 teaspoons caster sugar

300 ml/½ pint *cachaça*

1 With a sharp knife cut the limes into quarters and remove the coarse central membranes. Slice the lime quarters into small, even chunks.

2 Put the ice cubes into a plastic bag, place on a chopping board and reduce them to splinters using a rolling pin or similar.

3 Combine the limes and sugar in mortar (skilful barmen do all this in individual glasses in front of you), pounding them together. Add the *cachaça* and crushed ice and shake well, preferably in a cocktail shaker or in a jug with the top covered. Don't use a blender – the pieces of lime must remain whole.

4 Serve in glasses you have chilled in the freezer.

Opposite *White Rum Sour and Passion Fruit Cocktail (page 119)*

Coconut Milk Shake

Refresco de Côco

A deceptively simple, cooling and nourishing drink for a hot day. This recipes uses skimmed milk, which is light and refreshing, although semi-skimmed or full fat milk is just as tasty if more filling. **Makes 4 drinks**

1 coconut

1 litre/1¾ pints skimmed milk

caster sugar to taste

1 Pierce two of the three holes at the base of the coconut and pour out the liquid (*água de côco*), reserving it. Strain the liquid in a sieve to remove fibres and dust which fall from the shell.

2 Break open the coconut using a hammer or other implement. Cut the shards of flesh from the shell. Cut the hard brown skin from the coconut flesh, then grate, using a food mixer with a grater attachment to spare your fingers.

3 Heat the milk, without boiling, and stir in the grated coconut. Remove from the heat and put aside to infuse for 40 minutes. Pour the coconut-flavoured milk through a cloth into a bowl, tightening the cloth to extract all the juice, like wringing out a T-shirt. Combine with the *água de côco*.

4 Add a little caster sugar to taste, stirring to dissolve, and add a little water to dilute the drink. Chill well. Serve from the fridge with ice cubes.

Limeade

Limonada Suissa

Limonada suissa is the name given in Brazil to the national drink of limeade, the pungent green limão *being the nearest citrus fruit they have to lemon.* **Makes 6–8 drinks**

1 Pare the zest from 1 lime. Put the zest in a saucepan with the sugar and 125 ml/4 fl oz water and bring to the boil, stirring until the sugar has dissolved. Remove from the heat and leave to cool completely. Remove the lime zest.

8 limes

250g /9 oz caster sugar

2 Squeeze the juice from the limes and add to the sugar syrup. Chill.

3 Serve from the fridge, adding crushed ice and water to dilute to taste.

Coconut and Pumpkin Preserve

Cocada com Abóbora

Brazil has many unconventional preserves not found in Europe, such as sugared beetroot, sweetened carrot and many based on pumpkin, a native vegetable. Unusually pumpkin is combined with coconut in this preserve. **Makes about 2 x 450 g/1 lb jars**

about 250 g/9 oz *abóbora* (or use butternut or kabocha squash) to give 150 g/5 oz flesh

500 g/1 lb 2 oz sugar

2 cloves

150 g/5 oz freshly grated coconut or 125 g/4½ oz desiccated coconut

1 Peel the *abóbora* and remove the fibres and seeds. Cut the flesh into small pieces.

2 Bring 1 litre/1¾ pints of water to the boil in a saucepan. Add the sugar and stir to dissolve.

3 Add the *abóbora* and the cloves. Quickly bring to the boil and cook until the *abóbora* breaks down into a purée, stirring to avoid sticking or burning. When it thickens, stir in the coconut and simmer for 10 more minutes to allow the coconut flavours to combine with the pumpkin.

Caramelized Coconut Preserve

Dissolve 600 g/1 lb 5 oz sugar in 250 ml/9 fl oz water. Off the heat stir in 150 g/5 oz freshly grated coconut or 125 g/4½ oz desiccated coconut, then simmer on a low heat for 10 minutes. Leave to cool.

White Coconut Preserve

Make the Caramelized Coconut Preserve using milk instead of water and flavouring it with 2–3 cloves.

Guava Paste

Goiabada

*The acidic, highly scented guava, varying from raw green to pretty yellow and pink,
is a very popular fruit in Brazil and is used in conserves, jellies, mousses and drinks.
A thick jellied paste of guava is usually found on the breakfast table to be eaten with
a slice of cheese, perhaps the squeaky, fresh white cheese of Minas Gerais. Goiabada
is a cousin of the Spanish* mermelada, *or quince paste, which is also popular in Brazil.*

Makes about 500 g/1 lb 2 oz

1 Cut off the skins of the guavas and scrape out the pips. Push the pulp
through a fine sieve. You should be left with about 500 g/1 lb 2 oz puréed
pulp. Weigh out an equal amount of sugar.

1 kg/2¼ lb ripe guavas

about 500 g/1 lb 2 oz sugar

butter for greasing

2 Put the sugar in a large pan and add 125 ml/4 fl oz water. Bring to the
boil, stirring to dissolve the sugar, then boil to the soft ball stage (115°C/
239°F on a sugar thermometer). You can test by dipping a teaspoon of the
boiling sugar syrup into a bowl of cold water; if the syrup can be shaped
into a small ball, it is ready.

3 Add the guava purée and stir with the sugar syrup until the mixture
comes away from the sides of the pan. Remove from the heat. Spread on
a buttered baking tray and leave to cool.

4 Once cold and set, cut into squares and wrap in greaseproof paper to
store in airtight tins.

I would like to thank the many Brazilian friends who have, over the years, shared with me their love of Brazil and introduced me to its vibrant culture: in particular Marcia Magnavita Marques da Silva and her family; Betty Chiaratti, Margaret van Peterkin, David and Zelia Edwards. Among others who have offered inspiration and information: chef Jean-Yves Poirey and Teresa Pedruzzi of Le Meridien, Copacabana, Rio de Janeiro, and chef Adauto Rodrigues of the São Paulo Hilton, and in London, Andrew and Alberina Hunton of Sabor do Brasil, Highgate. At the Brazilian Embassy in London, Tovar da S. Nunes and Maria Graça-Fish.

I owe a special debt to Elisabeth Lambert Ortiz, the food writer most influential in awakening us to the Latin-American culinary world in books such as *The Book of Latin-American Cooking* (Penguin) and *The Flavours of Latin America* (Latin-American Bureau, London). Among Brazilian books which convey the unique spirit of the North-east are *A Culinaria Baiana*, produced by the SENAC cookery school in Salvador de Bahia, and Darwin Brandão's *A Cozinha Baiana*.

I would also like to thank the Conran Octopus team for their warm support, managing editor Kate Bell, art director Leslie Harrington and copy editor Norma MacMillan, as well as Suzannah Gough and Jenni Muir, who first invited me to write this book.

And finally, thanks to my wife, Heather, and my children, Alex and Georgia, who share my passion for all things Brazilian.

PUBLISHER'S ACKNOWLEDGEMENTS

The publisher would like to thank the following photographers for their kind permission to reproduce the photographs in this book:

6–7 James Davis Travel Photography; 38–39 Anthony Blake Photo Library/Guy Moberly; 60–61 Travel Ink/Charlie Marsden; 84–85 Carlos Freire/Hutchison Library; 112–113 Sue Cunningham/SCP

Also thanks to Hilary Bird for the index, Susanna Tee for recipe testing and Sarah Widdecombe for proofreading.